# THE 3-DEEP BETTING SYSTEM FOR COLLEGE FOOTBALL

*Turning Fish Into WiseGuys*

Raleigh Randall

✽ ✽ ✽

Copyright 2019 by WinningBetter.com

All rights reserved. No part of this publication may be reproduced, distributed, or transmitted in any form or by any means without written permission.

* * *

Contact support@winningbetter.com for further information.

* * *

The 3-Deep Betting System for College Football / Raleigh Randall -- 1st ed.

* * *

# CONTENTS

Title Page
Copyright
The Ideal Audience for this Book
About the Author
Forward
Here's How the 3-Deep Betting System Works
The 3-Deep Betting System Online Course
Imagine Yourself Almost Doubling Your Money Every Year

| | |
|---|---|
| Planning to Lose Is the Foundation for Winning | 1 |
| A Definition for the Money Line That I Can Understand | 7 |
| The Skill Level of the Players is the Most Important Factor in the 3-Deep Betting System | 9 |
| Where the Data to Assess the Skill Level of Each Player Comes From | 13 |
| The Most Important Source Available for Assessing College Football Skills | 14 |
| The College Football Depth Charts and Rosters | 16 |
| Where and How to Get the Skill Scores | 18 |
| What to Do With the Rating Data When You Get It | 22 |
| How to Put the Depth Chart Data Together | 25 |
| What It Means to Assess the Depth of a Team | 29 |

| | |
|---|---|
| How to Assess the Data to Determine the Depth of a Team | 32 |
| How to Evaluate Coaching Week-by-Week | 34 |
| Tying It All Up Into an Efficient System | 37 |
| How to Bet the Money Line | 41 |
| Conclusion | 42 |

# DISCLAIMER

This book is not a substitute for the financial advice of investment counselors, CPAs, or attorneys. Use caution and always consult your accountant, lawyer, or professional advisor before acting on this or any information related to a lifestyle change, your business, or finances.

You are the variable and accountable for the results you get in your life; by reading this book, you agree not to hold the author or publisher liable for your decisions, actions, or outcomes, under any circumstances.

A diligent effort has been made to ensure that the information in this book is accurate. However, the author and publisher do not guarantee the accuracy of the information, text, and graphics contained herein due to the rapidly changing nature of science, research, or known or unknown facts. The author and publisher do not hold any responsibility for errors, omissions or contrary interpretation of the the subject matter here. This book is presented solely for educational purposes.

# THE IDEAL AUDIENCE FOR THIS BOOK

If you consistently lose money betting on college football, this is for you.

If you hide your bets from other people because you don't want to get caught, this is for you.

If you're frustrated because the whole thing feels like a scam, this is for you.

If you just want to consider this method as a viable part of your investment strategy, this is for you.

# ABOUT THE AUTHOR

I've been a risk-taker all my life, with stock market speculation, futures trading, betting on college football games, and as an entrepreneur. I'm the creator of the *3-Deep Betting System for College Football.*

I'm a player, just like you, and I haven't always been a winner. As I developed this method, I amazed myself. I had a hunch that betting college football could be simpler and truer to what really mattered. Well, I was right. Like you, I don't believe a lot of things I see and read. I've been burned a lot . . . lost a lot of money and time. This won't happen to you here.

My method to win consistently when betting on college football is not a big secret at all! It's at the core of the process that made Nick Saban, Bill Belichick, and Kirby Smart consistent winners! So, let me tell you how it can give you the peace of mind every winner has.

# FORWARD

If you've ever played football, or any competitive game for that matter, what's the first thing on your mind? If you're about to go into battle, it's not whether your team is consistently covering the spread or even whether the game is on artificial turf or grass, home or away. It's this: *Am I going to be able to beat that dude across from me? Is he going to make me his bitch for the next couple of hours? Can I suck it up and compete with this freak?*

Belichick is famous for his mantra, "just do your job." But your job is to beat the hell out of your opponent, and that might not be easy.

Winners are better than their competition! **Let that sink in.** They don't win because they play on grass or artificial turf. They don't win because they're a dog on the road or a big home favorite. They don't win because the Dow Jones Industrial Average is up or down. They win because they're better than their opponent!

Now, all of a sudden this might sound too simple for you. I know you're used to plugging in a team's record, their schedule, passing yards, yards per attempt, rushing yards, yards per carry, sacks, negative passing plays, field surface, home field, away record, how often they cover... shall I go on?

NO! You don't need to know all that to win consistently.

> *To Win Consistently, You Need to Assess Talent and Depth Accurately and Know How to Factor in Coaching Properly . . . That's It!*

THAT'S ALL -- 3 things!

I'll teach you to do that, and you will begin winning

. . . and keep winning, with this simple process.

* * *

Apparently, most people think what I'm going to teach you is hard to do; so they don't do it. That's why you'll have an edge with this system. It would be hard if I hadn't done all the grunt work for you. I've already set up the system so that it's easy to get the information you need and use it to make every season a profitable one. It's not only easy, but fun.

## *Don't Worry About The Learning Curve . . .*

. . . because we do it for you, if you want to use our automated system!

> *Even though this book might entice you to do that, you don't need to. Everything you need to develop your own system is contained in the book.*

If you don't want to learn a new system, just follow our picks and look forward to a winning season.

* * *

If you like learning, but don't want to spend a lot of time on your handicapping... use our automated tools. We've set it all up for you. You can pick your winners with two clicks of a mouse.

❊ ❊ ❊

If you want to do it all yourself, we give you step-by-step instructions and training for every aspect of the system.

# HERE'S HOW THE 3-DEEP BETTING SYSTEM WORKS

First of all, we don't bet the spread; we bet the MoneyLine. We know that making a bet on the point spread doesn't exactly offer a level playing field. That pesky 10 percent commission most sports books charge gets in the way, forcing bettors to win at least 52.3 percent of the time to see any profit. But the MoneyLine is not the secret. It's not *that* simple. We assess team talent. We assess team depth. And we factor in coaching success. Then we make the call.

❊ ❊ ❊

We assess the skill level at each position. We have a proprietary, proven, and efficient way of doing that.

❊ ❊ ❊

We assess the team depth at each position, going 3-deep on the players that are in the depth chart.

\* \* \*

We assess coaching success during the season, game by game; and then we adjust our position/depth score.

\* \* \*

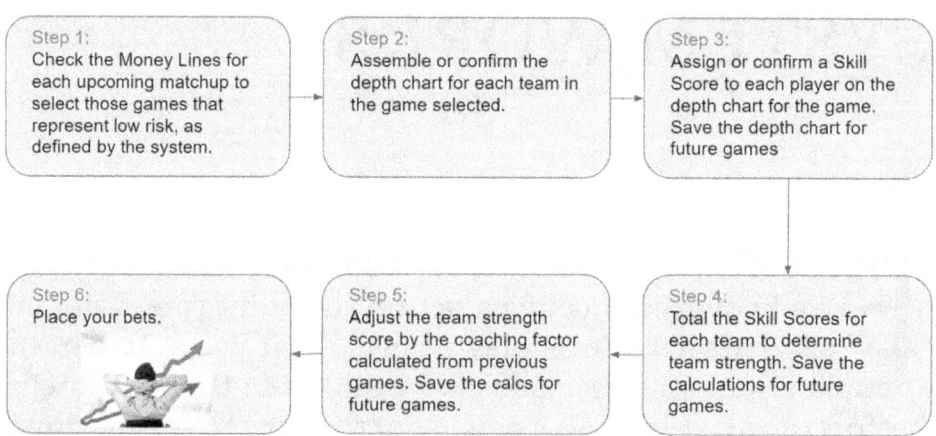

## And here's the last piece of the puzzle!

When you engage in any gambling activity, your most important skill is survival. New gamblers must survive until they learn how to last forever - until they learn enough to avoid a bust. With our training, we take care of the learning curve for you.

When you play in the futures market, as I did, you face some of the fiercest competition you will ever meet. You must learn how to manage your money, and the same is true in this arena. *My experience in futures trading became a gold mine of lessons for sports betting.*

You can win 80% of the time and lose everything, because you made stupid bets. This is a lesson many people never learn.

So, betting strategy is a big part of the 3-Deep Betting System. In this system, conservative bets produce monster returns. As a student of my method, you'll never have to worry about a bust.

# THE 3-DEEP BETTING SYSTEM ONLINE COURSE

A s I said earlier in the book, we have an online course that might suit you better as a learning platform. However, everything you need to know is contained in this book.

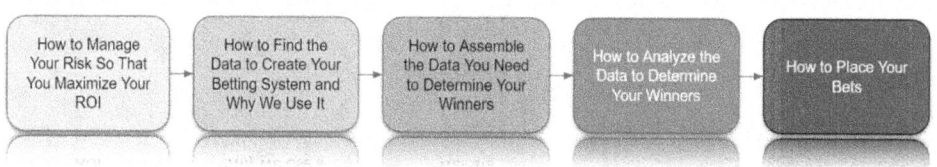

*A Step-by-Step Procedure to Assess Every Team's Skill Level, Position by Position*

The data is out there. You just need to know where and how to efficiently get it. By the way, this data didn't exist until the year 2000, and it wasn't taken seriously until at least five years later.

※ ※ ※

*A Step-by-Step Process to Assess Every Team's Depth Level, Position by Position*

We make sure you're looking at the depth of talent for each position on the day that the game is played.

※ ※ ※

*A Step-by-Step Method to Assess Coaching Success for Each Game and What It Means for the Next One*

No one looks at this factor like we do.

※ ※ ※

This simple system works so well, that our performance dwarfs that of the most successful handicappers on the Internet.

Compare these two statements!

This is a quote from a major sports picks website:

> We published a list of names who have excelled over the past several years. This combines every pick they released including money lines, sides, and totals. You'll find some big names on this list, but also a few that might surprise you. With this large of a sample size, don't discount anyone listed below.
>
> **[Called the *World's Top 10 Rated Sports Handicapping Experts*, they averaged a 4.5% ROI, with a 53.6% win rate.]**

> *"Since we began publishing our calls in 2017, we have a documented record of **winning 57% of our picks, generating an average 72% annual ROI**. Our longest losing streak in two years has been two weeks. You can see it for yourself on our Facebook page. You can also download a spreadsheet of that record from our website."*  - Raleigh Randall

# IMAGINE YOURSELF ALMOST DOUBLING YOUR MONEY EVERY YEAR

What would that mean to you? How would that affect your sleep, your family life, your peace of mind, your future? Gambling may have been your downfall in the past, but your past is not your future.

※ ※ ※

You may know that Billy Walters has employed an army of "consultants" to feed him data and information on each college football weekend to make his picks. Billy became the most successful player in the history of sports betting by being so thorough in his analysis.

I'm no Billy Walters, and this system doesn't come close to the complexity of his. It doesn't even come close to the complexity of most handicapping processes.

It's simple by comparison. On the first pass, it may seem too simple to you. Don't be fooled by its simplicity. You cannot argue with a 57% win rate on bets placed and a 72% ROI.

So, let's get started.

# PLANNING TO LOSE IS THE FOUNDATION FOR WINNING

**W**ithout a sound plan for managing your risk, you will never be a successful speculator. As a futures trader of commodities and currencies, I have studied more than a hundred books, white papers, courses, and case studies on speculation. Not one fails to stress the importance of risk management.

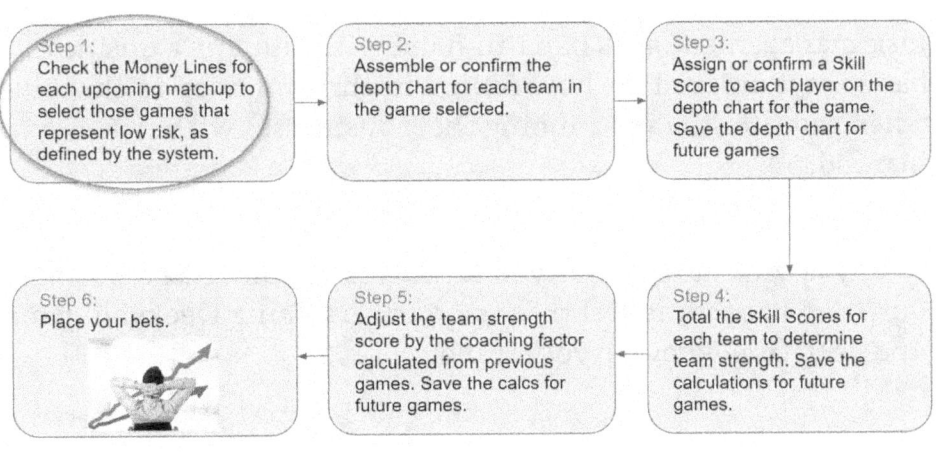

Raleigh Randall

I know from practical experience as a winner and loser in the futures market, that managing your risk will determine whether you survive and prosper.

I also know that from betting on college football games.

Without a risk management plan, you will be in high cotton one week and in the toilet the next. If that is what draws you to the betting game, you probably won't like this system.

You won't like it because there are no highs and lows with the method. It is just a steady stream of modest returns, week after week, that compound into monster returns by the end of the year.

Our theory is that you can absolutely control the risk with the discipline you will learn in this process. We will forgo the excitement of the peaks and valleys in favor of slowly getting rich.

## Treat This Like a Business

Risk management goes hand-in-hand with running a business. It has always amazed me how folks will throw money to the wind when gambling, while running their businesses with risk always in mind.

So, my advice here is that you treat this venture like a business. Don't let it become just a fun and entertaining weekend game. And keep risk always in your mind.

## This is the way we do it.

We manage the risk associated with college football betting by doing three things:

    1) betting the Money Line rather than the spread

    2) never betting a favorite that has a risk/reward ratio greater than 3.3 to 1

    3) never placing a bet on a favorite unless the pick has at least a 25% margin in Team Skill Score

## Choosing the Money Line

If you have some experience, you know that sophisticated bettors often make a choice between the money line and the spread. Less experienced gamblers may have never heard of the money line. Search the internet and you will find mountains of arguments for doing one thing or the other.

I've spent a great deal of time trying to figure out why I could never consistently beat the spread. Maybe you have, too. All I know is that I've heard from many experienced gamblers that they don't know anyone who consistently makes money betting the spread, including themselves. And that's why I finally turned to the money line. It simply made more sense to me.

Both have their inherent risk, but that risk is expressed by the bookmakers in different ways. I've just simplified it for myself by sticking with the money line, found success with it, and am now teaching it to others. I suppose, then, that it has less risk for me because I understand it better.

✻ ✻ ✻

Raleigh Randall

I'm not the only one with a preference for the money line, though. Consider this:

Chad Millman, of ESPN's *Insider* blog, met Mike Wohl at the MIT Sloan Sports Analytics Conference. Mike was the MBA graduate student coordinator for the panel Chad was on about the world of sports betting today.

The SSAC has a lot of star power — Jeff Van Gundy, Mark Cuban, Bill Simmons — but the gambling enthusiasts do not come for the panelists; they come for the info. Most folks sitting out there, especially the students, probably have an iPad stuffed in their backpack that contains the next great system for betting on sports.

It's at places like Sloan, and all the other brainiac grad institutions, where the real revolution in sports wagering is taking place. Chad often talks about the middle ground that exists between the sharps who do this for a living and the squares who can't.

Mike Wohl sent Chad his Sloan independent study called "The Missing Asset Class." Lo and behold, Wohl found the asset in college football money line bets.

Wohl found his advantage in betting the money lines for college football teams that were favored by 20-25 points. He wrote in his paper: "There were 376 games in the last six seasons (approximately 62 per season or approximately 4.5 per week) that had spreads of between 20.0 and 25.0. Of those 376 games, 94.95 percent of the favorites won the game outright."

Here's why that is so significant:

First of all, that simple strategy - betting the favorite when the spread is 20-25 points - returned an average 12.25% over 376 games from 2006 to 2011. Imagine what he could have done by adding in our factors of Skill Scores, Depth Charts, and Coaching. The average return in the stock market was 4.7% during that same time period.

We bet favorites and dogs with the 3-Deep Betting System. When we see favorites with no more than a 3.3 to 1 risk ratio, we take the bet if the proprietary Skill Score we calculate is at least 25% greater for the favorite than the dog (this is another risk-containment strategy).

The point is this: If a favorite has a 25% greater team Skill Score than the underdog, the favorite is almost always going to have a spread of 20-25. According to the research, that's a winner 95% of the time.

Now, I created this system before Mike did his research; but my method jibes with some serious research. It substantiates our strategy.

## *Containing Risk to a 3.3:1 Ratio*

There's a more detailed explanation of the money line in a following chapter, but this is what I mean by "containing risk to a 3.3 to 1 ratio":

When we bet an underdog with the money line, we will be betting $100 to win $150, for example. On the other hand, when we are betting a favorite we will be betting $150 to win $100.

"Containing risk to a 3.3 to 1 ratio" means that we never bet more than $330 on a favorite in order to win $100. It's as simple as that.

Our process for determining winners is so much more accurate than the most prevalent methods in the betting community, it gives us an edge. That edge often enables us to pick underdogs that may have more than a 3.3 to 1 payoff. It also enables us to accept a risk as much as 3.3 to 1 on favorites that are substantiated by our method.

In fact, we have many winning bets that return more than 3X our money, but we have none where we have lost more than 3X our money. For example (in 2017 and 2018), our largest loss was -$270 while our largest gain was +$525. Our average loss was $119, and our average win was $141; plus, we had 32% more wins than losses. This imbalance produces winning seasons, and it is simply due to risk containment.

## Why 3.3 to 1?

This number is from empirical evidence. We looked back over our records and saw that we have been able to risk as much as $330 to win $100 and determined that 3.3 to 1 is the optimal risk ceiling for this system.

**Note:** We always monitor our system's performance. This ratio is the optimum now, but it could change based on back-tests. If it does change, we will announce it to our students.

# A DEFINITION FOR THE MONEY LINE THAT I CAN UNDERSTAND

Google "money line" or "moneyline" and you will find more posts and pages about it than you can read in a lifetime. Many of them are complicated and don't make much sense. Many of them are simple and easy to understand. I'll try to make it simple. If you want to dig into it more, go to Google.

When you bet the money line, you are betting that one team or another will win or lose straight up. There is no spread, as in plus or minus 2.5 points, that you routinely hear about. So, forget about the spread.

However, the money line has its own odds; but they're expressed in a different way.

When betting the money line, you will find that each team has an amount of money assigned to it; and that money amount will be negative for the favorite and positive for the dog. Let's say that Notre Dame is favored over Georgia. The money line will say "Notre Dame -$150, for example." This means that if you bet on Notre Dame, you must bet $150 (or some multiple thereof). If Notre Dame wins, you win only $100 (or some multiple thereof).

For that same game, the bookies might say "Georgia +$150." This means that if you bet on Georgia, you can bet $100 to win $150.

*** * ***

You will see in our record of 2017-2018 plays that our bets in this account were all in $100 amounts when betting on underdogs and greater than $100, but no more than $330, when betting on favorites. Over the course of two years, this minimal betting returned $2,290. We risked no more than $770 in any one week during that time.

However, you may be able to bet much more. For example, if you had a stash of $77,000 rather than $770, your annual return would have been $114,500. A bankroll of $770,000 would have generated more than a million dollars a year in income, etc. This represents a viable business for many people and illustrates why risk containment becomes so important.

# THE SKILL LEVEL OF THE PLAYERS IS THE MOST IMPORTANT FACTOR IN THE 3-DEEP BETTING SYSTEM

The skill level of each player is the most important factor in our system. There was a time when the rating system for high school football players' skills wasn't taken very seriously. In fact, it didn't exist in any formal and usable way until the year 2000. College coaches all talked it down, publicly claiming that they paid no attention to the ratings. But privately, they were all ears.

By the way, I use the term 'skill' rather than 'talent' for what I think is a good reason. A player can be blessed with talent but never develops that talent. I believe a less talented player can become more skilled than one with the blessing of more talent, because he works harder to develop the skill. The rating system, therefore, is an assessment of skill -- not talent.

We are now in an era where this rating system is acknowledged universally by college coaches as sound and valuable. They use it extensively to identify and recruit the most skilled players. If it didn't work, they wouldn't regard it so highly.

There are volumes of evidence that it is important to the game and winning, but let's look at just one compelling fact as proof: Nick Saban, as of 2019, has recruited better than any other college coach in America in the past decade according to the *247Sports Composite List of Top Football Recruits*. Guess which college has more active NFL players than any other as of 2019? Alabama!

It is indisputable that you must have more skill among your players than your opponents to win consistently -- with very few exceptions. It is an absolute no-brainer.

*But, let's get real!*

The age of high school players makes it very difficult to scout them. You are grading seventeen to eighteen year-olds whose bodies are not fully developed. They need to add weight and muscle mass, and in some cases they haven't reached their full height. Their maturity level is still rather low, because they are technically still kids. It's hard to predict someone's full potential when they're so young.

Players at the high school level are extremely rough around the edges. In most cases they do not have the best of coaches, and they develop plenty of bad habits. It then takes coaches like Nick

Saban, Kirby Smart, and Dabo Swinney to clean them up when they reach the college level. A quarterback coming out of high school has not faced some of the best man coverages possible. The pass rushers have not faced some of the best college offensive linemen. It's high school; the competition is a lower level of difficulty, and the stats and play can look better than they really are.

Nevertheless, today's high school scouting system generates the best information available about skill levels. There are thousands of scouts around the country. There are hundreds, if not thousands, of football camps, combines, and retreats churning out hard, unbiased stats on every skill important to winning football. It's the best we have, and it certainly means more than many of the factors that the average handicapper considers.

Raleigh Randall

*Recruiting rankings and NFL Draft picks go hand and hand.*

Yes, the rating assigned to players is three to five years out from when a player actually enters the draft. But few measures predict a prospect's NFL future better than their high school ranking.

Five-stars, in general, are eventually drafted 50-plus percent of the time. Three-star players, meanwhile, make it at a rate of around five percent. The data shows, by and large, that the recruiting industry does a good job identifying skill level, even half a decade away from when those players will land in the pros.

If it is such an accurate predictor for the pros, doesn't it make sense that it is even more accurate for college play?

# WHERE THE DATA TO ASSESS THE SKILL LEVEL OF EACH PLAYER COMES FROM

We find this data in the *247Sports Composite List of Top Football Recruits* (find it at 247sports.com). This page has the player's name, position, height/weight, rating, and team. For now, we are interested only in:

    1) name

    2) position

    3) rating

    4) team

Raleigh Randall

# THE MOST IMPORTANT SOURCE AVAILABLE FOR ASSESSING COLLEGE FOOTBALL SKILLS

There's no doubt about it, college football recruiting determines the success or failure of any program. And the *247Sports Composite Rating* is the industry's most comprehensive and unbiased prospect ranking source. This list is now widely regarded by media and college football personnel as the gospel when it comes to college football team recruiting rankings. So to make this assessment, we use the *247Sports Composite List of Top Football Recruits*.

247Sports uses a proprietary algorithm that compiles rankings and ratings listed in the public domain by the major media recruiting services. It includes the lists from Scout, Rivals, ESPN.com, and its own. It converts average industry ranks and ratings into a linear composite index capping at 1.0000, which indicates a consensus No.1 prospect across all services.

In 2016-17, the National Federation of State High School Sports counted 1,039,079 high school football players nationwide. There were approximately:

30 five-stars

400 four-stars

1,300 three-stars

1,900 two-stars

... for a total of about 3,500 high school football players rated by 247Sports each year.

So, the *247Sports Composite List of Top Football Recruits* is our database for assessing skill levels.

However, getting this data can be tedious and cumbersome. So, we've simplified it for you in our online course. Each year we compile a list of more than 16,000 high school players that have been scouted and assigned ratings over the previous four years. These are the players that make up the squads of the 130 teams we evaluate each week.

This is the first component in your system.

# THE COLLEGE FOOTBALL DEPTH CHARTS AND ROSTERS

The previous lesson explained the factor that is at the core of our system. That core factor is what the *247Sports Composite List of Top Football Recruits* calls *Rating*. We assign that Rating factor to each player who shows up in the depth chart for the game we are playing. In our system, we call it *Skill Score*.

So, the next question is where is the depth chart and how do I get it. This lesson will take you through that process.

The College Football Depth Charts and Rosters are published and updated weekly by *Ourlads' NFL Scouting Services*. Each week they publish the depth charts for every one of the 130 teams in the Division 1 conferences.

# The 3-Deep Betting System for College Football

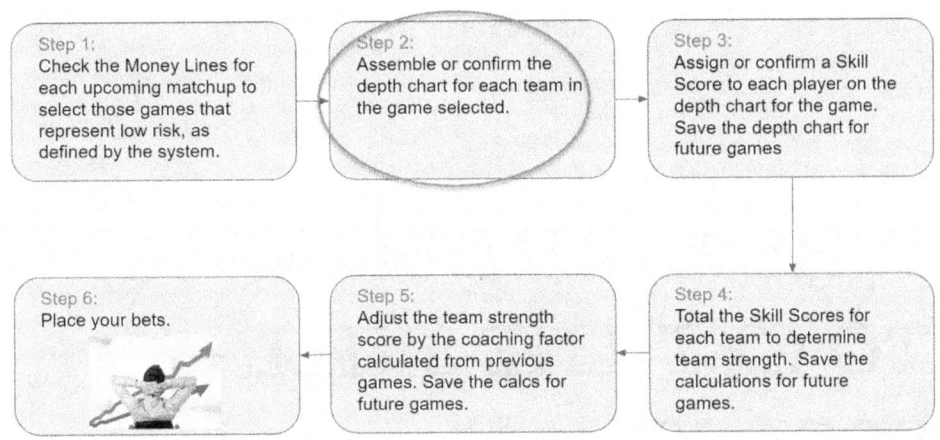

**Attention:** *If you are looking at this data or putting it together for your system during the off-season, beware! Depth chart and rosters data won't be updated until just before the season starts. You will be receiving inaccurate data until then.*

**Looking Ahead:** You will be recording the players' Skill Scores onto the depth chart.

# WHERE AND HOW TO GET THE SKILL SCORES

Search Google for the player. Click the link in the Search results that says, for example, *Frank Coppet - 247Sports*.

This is what the Google Search results page looks like when you search for a player:

# The 3-Deep Betting System for College Football

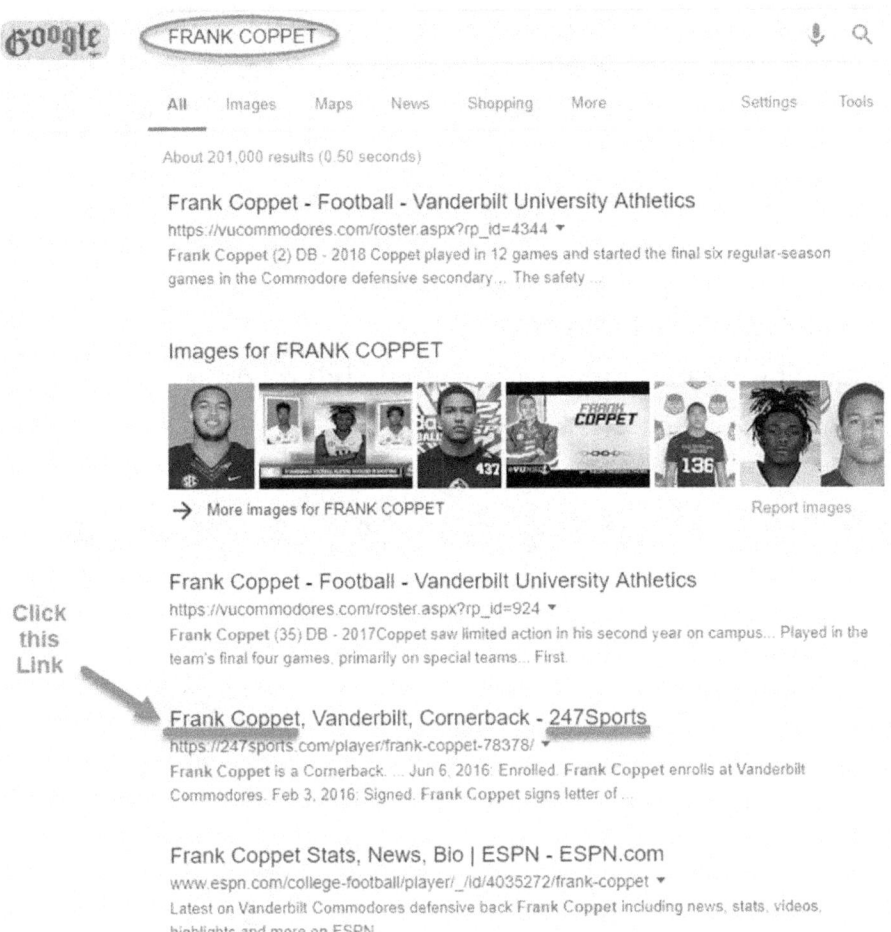

If the player has been rated relatively high by 247Sports, there will be a Google link (like you see in the above graphic) on page 1 of the search results. If the player has a relatively low rating, you may see other links for him, but not a 247Sports link. This means that the player probably has a rating less than .8000, and Google does not have a link for him on the first page.

There are other reasons why you may not see links for the player you're trying to find. This happens most often with players who have common names like John Smith. It also happens quite often when players have celebrity names like Dwayne Johnson. If you run into this, change your search from *Frank Coppet* to something like *Frank Coppet Vanderbilt* or *Frank Coppet football*. If this doesn't work, go to the 247Sports website and search for the player there.

## How to Search the 247Sports Website When You Need To

1) Navigate to the 247Sports website.
2) Select the year the player graduated high school.
3) Click the Search icon to find the player.

Whether you find the player through a Google search or from a search within the 247Sports website, the page in the exhibit below is the next page you will see.

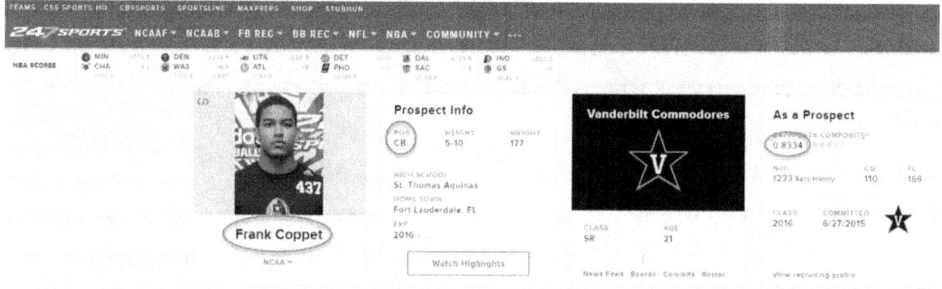

The 3-Deep Betting System for College Football

This page has the information you need to develop your system.

From this page, you will record the player's name, his position, and the 247Sports rating.

**Note:** You will have to do this only once per year.

# WHAT TO DO WITH THE RATING DATA WHEN YOU GET IT

Your objective is to determine a Skill Score for the opponents of the matchup you plan to bet. To make that determination, you must compile a 3-deep depth chart for the teams you are evaluating.

The importance of the depth chart is that it enables you to know what the total Skill Score is for each team, based on the individual Skill Scores for each player on the depth chart for that day.

So, working backward from this objective, this is what you do:

1) Go to the College Football Depth Charts and Rosters page at www.ourlads.com.

2) Click on the Depth Chart link for the team you are evaluating.

*This will launch the depth chart for the team. These depth charts are updated each week on Wednesday for the upcoming games.*

*The depth charts do not have Skill Scores for the players listed. You'll have to insert these Skill Scores later. So, for now . . .*

3) Record the depth chart into a spreadsheet or some application that will allow you to add to the data and calculate a team Skill Score.

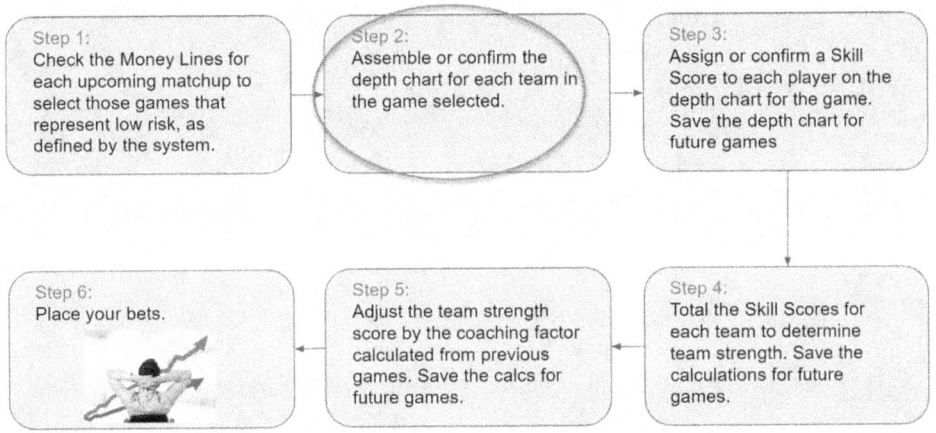

This is what my depth charts used to look like (before I automated and created my course) in an Excel spreadsheet:

Raleigh Randall

|    | A   | B                | C               | D                 | E      |
|----|-----|------------------|-----------------|-------------------|--------|
| 1  |     |                  |                 |                   |        |
| 2  | WR  | Riley Ridley     | Jayson Stanley  | Demetris Robertson |        |
| 3  |     | 0.9089           | 0.9081          | 0.9905            | 2.8075 |
| 4  | WR  | Jeremiah Holloman | Tyler Simmons  |                   |        |
| 5  |     | 0.9431           | 0.8822          |                   | 1.8253 |
| 6  | WR  | Terry Godwin     | Mecole Hardman  | Ahkil Crumpton    |        |
| 7  |     | 0.9879           | 0.991           | 0                 | 1.9789 |
| 8  | LT  | Andrew Thomas    | Cade Mays       |                   |        |
| 9  |     | 0.9791           | 0.9869          |                   | 1.966  |
| 10 | LG  | Solomon Kindley  | Ben Cleveland   |                   |        |
| 11 |     | 0.8408           | 0.9565          |                   | 1.7973 |
| 12 | OC  | Lamont Gaillard  | Trey Hill       |                   |        |
| 13 |     | 0.9367           | 0.9692          |                   | 1.9059 |
| 14 | RG  | Trey Hill        | Cade Mays       |                   |        |
| 15 |     |                  |                 |                   | 0      |
| 16 | RT  | Isaiah Wilson    | Kendall Baker   |                   |        |
| 17 |     | 0.9904           | 0.8997          |                   | 1.8901 |
| 18 | TE  | Isaac Nauta      | Charlie Woerner | Jackson Harris    |        |
| 19 |     | 0.9904           | 0.9386          | 0.9221            | 2.8511 |
| 20 | QB  | Jake Fromm       | Justin Fields   |                   |        |
| 21 |     | 0.9794           | 0.9998          |                   | 1.9792 |
| 22 | RB  | Elijah Holyfield | D'Andre Swift   | Brian Herrien     |        |
| 23 |     | 0.9297           | 0.9838          | 0.8489            | 2.7624 |

**Looking Ahead:** You will fill out this depth chart spreadsheet to compare it to the opponent's depth chart.

# HOW TO PUT THE DEPTH CHART DATA TOGETHER

You're almost there. When we get the depth chart assembled, we're in the home stretch of developing a full system.

1) Record the players' names listed in the Player 1, Player 2, and Player 3 columns in a manner that will allow you to record their respective Skill Scores next to them.

2) Assign a Skill Score to each player.

3) Save the depth chart for use in future weeks.

## Attention

*If you are looking at this data or putting it together for your system during the off-season, beware! Depth chart and rosters data won't be updated until just before the season starts. You will be receiving inaccurate data until then.*

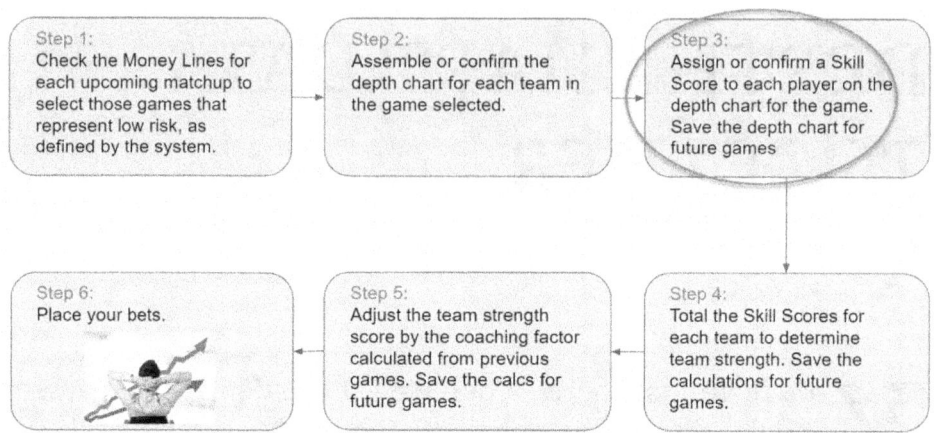

Sometimes this depth chart never changes; it stays the same all year. However, most do have some changes from week to week; but the changes are few. There is the possibility, though, that you will have to do this only once per year.

If you must use this team's depth chart for a future bet, you won't have to re-do it completely; you will only have to confirm it or make the small changes necessary.

You don't need the players' numbers or positions, and you don't need anything from the Player 4 and Player 5 columns on the *Ourlads* site.

# The 3-Deep Betting System for College Football

The above image serves to illustrate a point about why the depth chart is so important. As you can see, there are no names in the Player 3 column. You can conclude, then, that this team is lacking depth; and depth is an important component of a winning football team.

**Looking Ahead:** You will sum all the players' Skill Scores to generate a team Skill Score, and this score will be compared to the

Raleigh Randall

score of this team's opponent to pick your winners.

# WHAT IT MEANS TO ASSESS THE DEPTH OF A TEAM

As we said in the previous chapter, team depth is an all-important factor in winning football. Check the comments of coaches around the country every week. You'll hear, "we don't have enough depth" or something like "we have to develop more depth" or "we've got good depth on the offensive line." You never hear them say, "Well, we haven't been covering the spread very often; so, we have to work on that."

This is why we stress the importance of this factor in our system. Teams with a low level of depth will probably find most of their wins at the beginning of each season. As the season carries on and winds down, lack of depth kicks in. People often get hurt and tired playing this game. You constantly need "fresh legs," as they say.

Rather than looking at and evaluating just the starting lineup, we are evaluating all those players listed in the 3-deep depth chart. Their total Skill Score is what matters.

Raleigh Randall

## *Why We Do It That Way*

Teams may have players that start on the first team (the Ones), the main backups at the second level (the Twos), and maybe some players at the third level (the Threes).

Teams at the highest level of play usually have no more than a few Threes, and there are usually fewer Twos than Ones.

Just imagine a super-team with enough recruiting power to stack three levels of Ones, Twos, and Threes -- all with 22 players at each level. A vision of this makes it clear why depth is so important.

The more probable depth chart is 25 Ones, 22 Twos, and 3 Threes -- even at the highest levels of play.

Many times players show up on the depth chart more than once, because they back up more than one position (we don't count the dupes when calculating team Skill Scores). This happens more often among weaker teams, because they just don't have the personnel.

When we look at it this way and make our team Skill Score calculations by taking into account all three levels of depth, we make a more substantive evaluation of the team.

Everyone who has played the game knows that if you start against their starter and another guy comes in with "fresh legs," he can wear you out. This is especially tough on a team that is facing Twos and Threes with as much skill as the starters. It's a team game.

# HOW TO ASSESS THE DATA TO DETERMINE THE DEPTH OF A TEAM

By assembling the depth charts, we have an overview of how strong a team is depth-wise. Taking the simplest example with made-up numbers, let's suppose that Team A has 27 players in the Player 1 position. In the Player 2 position, they are thinner -- they have only 16 players. And there are no names in the Player 3 position.

Let's further suppose that each player has a Skill Score of .7500. When we total our Skill Score for Team A, we get a score of 36.75 (.7500 X 27 = 20.25 | .7500 X 16 = 12 | 20.25 + 16.5 = 36.75).

Team B might have 27 players in the Player 1 position, 26 players in the Player 2 position, and 6 players in the Player 3 position. If all their players had the same Skill Scores of .7500, their team score would be 44.25.

# The 3-Deep Betting System for College Football

In this scenario, you have to conclude that Team B will be stronger and more competitive than Team A.

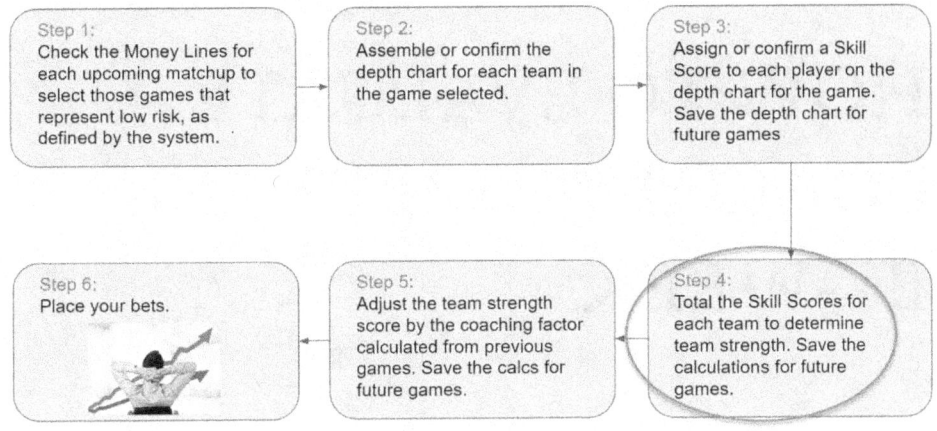

\* \* \*

1) At this point, then, we set up the depth chart in a spreadsheet and add the Skill Score for each player next to the player's name.

2) We then sum the Skill Scores for all players on the depth chart to get a total Skill Score for the team.

3) Now we save the revised depth chart for use in future games.

*Some players might have Skill Scores of 0, because they were not rated by the scouting services. Also, some players' names may have no skill score attached to them; because they show up more than once on the depth chart.*

# HOW TO EVALUATE COACHING WEEK-BY-WEEK

**What Goes Wrong?**

When Team A (with a Skill Score of 48) doesn't beat Team B (with a Skill Score of 43), something went wrong. So, where do we place the blame?

On paper, Team A should beat Team B; but, as they say, "We don't play these games on paper." If there was nothing else to consider except skill and depth levels, we would all be rich.

Over the course of 1,430 games among 130 teams in a season, our predictions will miss on almost 300 contests. Well, nobody's perfect!

## The 3-Deep Betting System for College Football

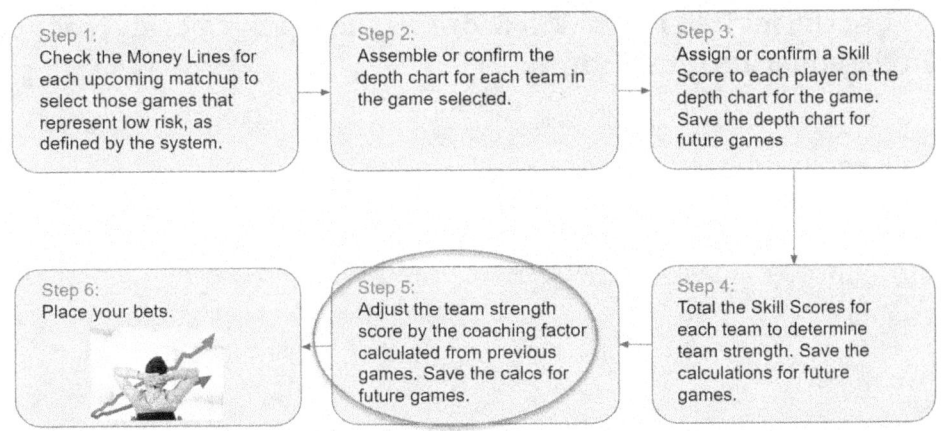

This is just a sample of what goes wrong in those 300 games:

> poor clock management

> wacky play calling

> too many turnovers

> too many penalties

> sideline confusion

> underestimating the competition

> coping with a hostile stadium

> lack of motivation (players weren't "ready")

Rather than fret over all these variables, we lump them all under *Coaching*. In fact, all these thing fall under the responsibility of the coaching staff. So, we factor this into our team evaluation in the following way:

1) If a team loses when it is supposed to win, subtract the average Skill Score for the team (Team Skill Score divided by players counted in the depth chart).

2) If a team wins when it is supposed to lose, add the average Skill Score of the team.

3) Use the revised team Skill Score on the next game, and keep it in the equation for season.

# TYING IT ALL UP INTO AN EFFICIENT SYSTEM

We bet both favorites and underdogs with this system. The steps below are the last steps to take before placing your bets.

*How to Bet the Favorites*

1) Go to *VegasInsider.com*. This page has all the D-1 matchups for the week and their money lines. The graphic below is an example of the page in season.

Raleigh Randall

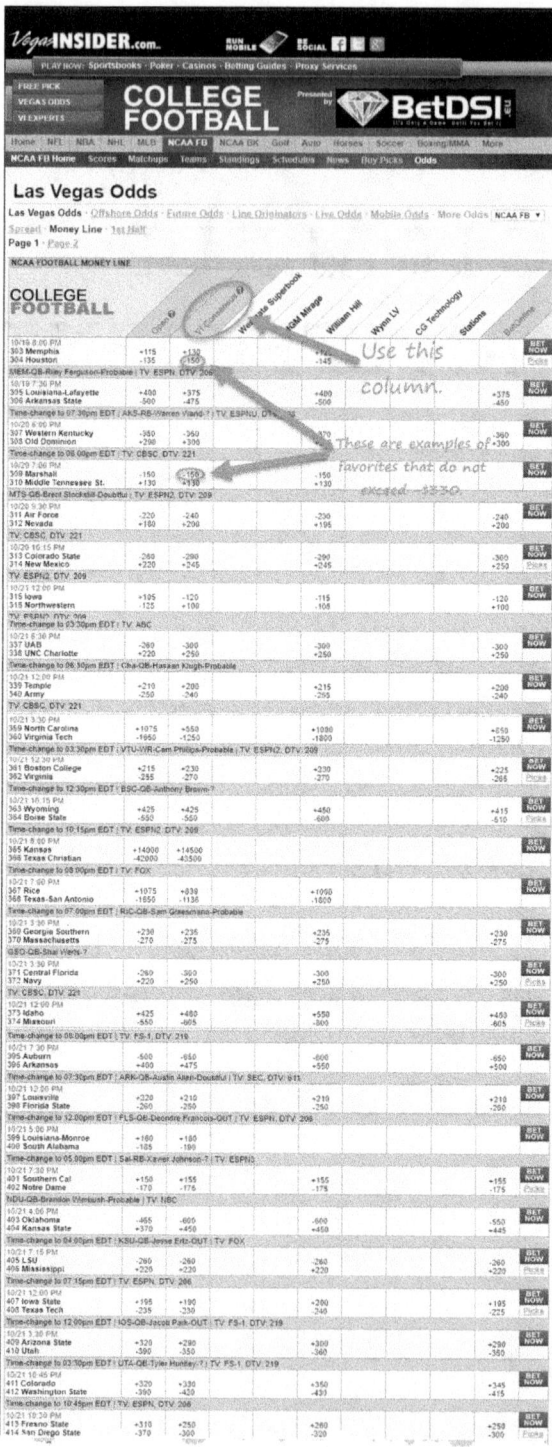

## The 3-Deep Betting System for College Football

2) Make a list of all the games that have a money line of no more than -$330 on the favorite. *A money line greater than -$330 means -$331 and up.* These are potential bets.

3) Assemble the depth charts for each team in the matchups to determine the total Skill Scores for each team.

4) If the team Skill Score for the favorite is at least 25% higher than the opponent, bet the game.

❊ ❊ ❊

Let's take an example from the page in the graphic above:

Houston vs. Memphis is a potential play.

Houston is the favorite.

The money line is -$150, less than -$330. You would need to bet $150 to win $100.

Let's suppose you know from your depth charts that the team Skill Score for Houston is 38.45, and the score for Memphis is 28.80. Is this a good bet, or not?

Yes, because 38.45 is almost 34% higher than 28.80.

This complies with our risk strategy of avoiding matchups where the difference in the two Skill Scores is less that 25%.

Bet it!

## *How to Bet the Underdog*

Betting on the underdog is more art than science, but our method goes like this:

1) Scan the list at VegasInsider.com, looking for the biggest money line amounts you can find for the dog.

2) Then calculate the team Skill Scores for each team in the contest.

3) When you find a matchup with an underdog that has a Skill Score higher than the favorite, bet it.

# HOW TO BET THE MONEY LINE

Placing your bets on the money line can be done in a thousand places on the Internet. Almost every game has a money line, in addition to a spread.

After New Jersey's Supreme Court victory in 2018, any state that wishes can legalize sports betting. At the time of my writing this in early 2019, 28 states had introduced bills to make it legal. Seven states already had full-scale legalized sports betting. That leaves only 15 states up in the air about it at this time.

In the meantime, the Internet has thousands of sites hosted offshore where millions of people place bets every day. Until it's legal in your state, you would be placing your bets through those sites.

Since the landscape of sports betting is changing every day and accelerating, I don't think it would be wise to be specific about how and where you should place your bets now. Just shop around as you would for any service.

# CONCLUSION

You now know a system based solidly on what matters most in winning football. The hocus-pocus of how often a team covers the spread, the type of field cover on which the game is being played, and any number of other "handicapping" factors is just that -- hocus-pocus.

This is not really a bold statement. Losers in the gambling community prove how difficult it is to win by betting on these factors every season... and they keep doing it, over and over.

If you follow the rules of this system, you can make a business out of betting on college football. I hope you enjoyed learning this, and I wish you the best of luck.

**PS**
If you found some value in my book, please leave a review on Amazon. And, by all means, if you found some shortcomings, leave your feedback there, too.

**PPS**
For more help and information on The 3-Deep Betting System for College football, visit *WinningBetter.com*.

www.ingramcontent.com/pod-product-compliance
Lightning Source LLC
Chambersburg PA
CBHW072208170526
45158CB00004BB/1798